VISION

KEN CAREY

This book is manufactured in the United states of
America. Distribution by The Talman Company.

The Talman Company
150 Fifth Ave.
New York, NY 10011

ISBN: 0-912949-03-1

First Printing, September 1985   15,000
Second Printing, March 1986   15,000
Third Printing, February 1987   10,000
Fourth Printing, September 1987   15,000

Cover Design: David Burke
Cover Photo: Hiroshi Haga

Table of Contents

INTRODUCTION

By Jean Houston

A few years ago friends began sending me a book. One month three copies would arrive, the following month five copies. By year's end I had acquired several dozen copies. My friends all assured me that the book was special and "had something." Indeed it had, for the book, *The Starseed Transmissions* by "Raphael," was perhaps the finest example of "channeled knowledge" I had ever encountered. It was at once both lyrical and hearty, offering a substantive view of the nature of the spiritual design and evolutionary purposes at work at depth dimensions of reality. It invited a co-evolutionary partnership without any particular ideological or sectarian base, although the Christian influence of the channeler was apparent. What was most impressive was the complexity and richness of ideas it provided, the sense of being in touch with the larger Pattern that was trying to enter into time. Who was it, I wondered, who had been the vehicle through which so deep and potent a communication was given. It turned out to be a young carpenter named Ken Carey who, with his wife and partner, Sherry, and their six children, was living a life reminiscent of the old frontier. This included building their house, growing their food, educating their children, and pretty much doing for themselves all the things which most people have long ceased to be able to do. It was very quiet and very beautiful in the remote part of Missouri where they lived, quiet enough that one could listen to the message of the wind in the trees, hear and understand birdsong, know what the stream said. After a while, a deeper message began to be heard. Ken listened and *The Starseed Transmissions* were born.

Ken has continued to listen and, in his growing seminars and retreats, taught others to do so also. This beautiful little book of visions is his latest receiving, and continues the theme begun in *The Starseed Transmissions* of our opportunity for co-creation with God at this most critical turning point in human history.

What is channeling and why is there so much channeled material appearing today? Channeling begins and ends in awareness, awareness of the enormous amounts of information coming to us all of the time. There is much to suggest that in pre-historic times we were much more generally aware of different cadences of information than we are now. A remarkable description of this level of awareness is given in Jean Auel's remarkable novel of the transition from Neanderthal to Homo sapien dominance 30,000 years ago. The following passage is from *The Valley of the Horses* and treats of the heroine's manner of paying attention to her environment:

> All her senses were alert. She listened for sounds of breathing or small scufflings; looked to see if there were any telltale signs of recent habitation; smelled the air for the distinctive odors of carnivorous animals, or fresh scat, or gamey meat, opening her mouth to allow her taste buds to catch the scent; let her bare skin detect any sense of warmth coming out of the cave; and allowed intuition to guide her as she noiselessly approached the opening. She stayed close to the wall, crept up on the dark hole, and looked in.

It is only a quarter turn from this extraordinary aware-ness of outward information to the sensing of unseen informa-tion, the taking in with the inward proprioceptors of the levels of information that may be coming to you from a flow pattern of electrons or the evolutionary pulse sounding in you from dimensions beyond those of ordinary space and time. Sensi-tives like Ken Carey, especially if they live in quiet natural settings, are not only more responsive to their environment, but are always enhancing their ability to sense or channel depth realms of Being as well.

Let us take a brief excursion into some speculations on the metaphysics and physics of what might be happening here. The phenomenon addressed from this point of view has its roots in the belief that psyche is invested in matter and there-fore matter can have access to psychic knowing. Thales of Miletus gave the first Western explanation in the 6th Century B.C. when he said that "all things are full of gods," meaning that a sort of psyche, a divine emanation, is both complemen-tary and co-extensive with matter and leads it towards larger realities. Plato wrote of the Forms or Archetypes implicit in all things, luring them to growth and becoming. Jesus speaks of the Kingdom Within and the immanence of the I AM nature of God in each person. The Sufi Islamic mystics refer to the *alam al mithal,* the *mundus imaginalis,* an intermediate uni-verse that is thought to be as ontologically real as the sensory empirical world and the noetic world of the intellect. It exists in a metageography and possesses extension and dimension as well as figure, color, and other features perceived by the senses. However, this world can be experienced only by those who exercise their psychospiritual senses, and, through this special form of imaginal knowing (which is very close, if not identical to channeling), gain access to a visionary world that is not unlike the *mundus archetypas* of Carl Jung.

The 17th Century philosopher Leibnitz declared the uni-verse to be made up of "monads" which are tiny units of mind, each of which mirrors (or channels) the universe from the perspective of its particular point of view. At the same time each monad is interrelated with every other, so that no monad can be changed without changing the other. The process philosophers of the 20th Century reflected this at depth, with Bergson saying that ultimate reality is an underlying web of connections and that the brain generally screens out the larger reality through its "cerebral reducing valves." Field theory and quantum physics gave further assent to these conjectures, especially Bell's 1964 theory which presents evidence to connect all spatially separated events. It tells us that no theory of reality compatible with quantum theory can require spatially separated events to be independent, but must allow for the interconnectedness of distant events in a way that differs from ordinary experience.

Lately, some of the new particle physicists are making some extraordinary claims that extend this hypothesis in ways that help illuminate the nature of channeling (although they would probably be the last to give the phenomenon credence). Physicists like Feynmann of Harvard, Wheeler at Princeton, and Jean Choron, the French physicist and writer, are suggesting that elementary particles of matter are actually particle micro-universes that, like regular universes, contain spaces which hold information in their spin or charge and evolve and increase it in non-decreasing negentropy. Since, according to Bell's theorem, electrons are able to exchange information at a distance with other electrons, the spin radiation effects seem to affect holonomically the spin effect of other electrons. An electron, furthermore, never forgets its informational content, its psychic charge as it were, whether the informational charge be that of a living person or a work of art. In other words, even when you die the entirety of your experience may be coded in the spin of electrons that make up your dust.

Choron uses the example of the visitor to Rameses the Second's mummy tuning into the life experiences of the Egyptian Pharaoh, since these are ubiquitous throughout the remaining electrons of his mummified body. Similarly, the experiences coded in the electrons of an object can just as well exchange information with your electrons as the electrons of a once living person. That is why we are literally bombarded with information about everything all of the time. Our "cerebral reducing valves" protect us from this avalanche of cosmic knowing. The council of six-headed Bratyridorians convening on a planet of Betelgeuse may be absolutely fascinating, but I'd rather not know about it. However, in situations of telepathy, psychometry, clairvoyance and channeling we use our own electrons as a transmitter/receiver in order to communicate with the electrons of another person or object or even cosmos. What we call the deeper or evolutionary impulses may be coming to us through the "black hole" vortex which is evidently contained in each electron, specifically the charged lepton, and through which we access other dimensions as well, that is, the dimensions of what physics refers to as n-dimensional space/time.

How we tune ourselves to being pulsed by other dimensions is a great open question, but however it happens, it seems reasonable at this time to assume that these sub-atomic dimensions or worlds operating at different frequencies are able to pulse their intention into our own. What we experience and label (out of our own cultural conditioning) as archetypes or gods or guides or even angels may reach us through the electron spin as it were. What they really are and where they are coming from God Only Knows. Be that as it may the universe bleeds through and we are diaphanous to its rhythms and knowings.

Seen from this perspective, channeled information is a by-product of this simultaneous-everywhere-matrix of reality. The channeler is he or she who is able to tune the electronic structure of his or her brain-mind to listen deeply for knowledge that gives the great patterns of reality, and then to structure them through the lenses of his or her own cultural conditioning so that these patterns make sense and wisdom in local space and time out of the immensities available for knowing.

One could explore at great length the many examples of channeling throughout history. The Old and New Testament are full of prophetic channelings. And oracles were sought as a main form of gaining deep knowledge or understanding throughout Europe and much of the rest of the world. For the most sophisticated of Greeks, in the high Hellenic civilization, final recourse to knowledge was often the oracle at Delphi who was thought to channel the gnosis of Apollo. Nostradamus channeled the pictures of the history of times to come. The great Swedish scientist Swedenborg saw through the surface world to multidimensional universes surrounding and supporting us. And of course William Blake painted and wrote out of the cornucopia of his ever-present visionary knowing. Throughout the shamanic cultures, the trance shaman consciously alters his attention on the spectrum of consciousness in order to access levels of knowing that are not usually available to ordinary states of consciousness. The works of Carlos Castaneda reflect this phenomenon as well as demonstrate the rigors of the training of the shamanic mind. For there is no question but that the nervous system and the brain have to be re-educated in order to open the doors of perception on the strange and beautiful country of channeled knowing. Otherwise one gets the great garbage heap of the unconscious, sanctified to the channeler and his duped disciples as the word of God. Indeed, a great deal of what passes for channeled information is just that—the flotsam and jetsam of the unconscious minds of inflated egos. What it lacks in clarity it more than makes up for in chutzpah!

In recent years, a growing number of people who would not normally be considered shamans or oracles or psychic egotists have begun to come forth with extraordinary channeled material. Edgar Cayce, the sleeping prophet who could diagnose at at distance people's ailments; David Spangler whose works *Emergence and Revelation* show a profound quality of depth knowing and prophetic insight; Jane Roberts and her Seth books with their skillful orchestration of the varieties of psychic knowings; and now the potent and potentiating work of Ken Carey—these are among the finest products of channeled information. Although each of these channelers reflects in some way their own cultural and religious bias (witness the recurring Christian themes in Cayce and Carey), they each speak to a vision and a gnosis deeper than any culture, more universal than any theology. And what they all receive is the message: IT'S TIME TO WAKE UP NOW! The human race is about to join a universe larger than our aspiration and richer than all our dreams. It is time to prepare ourselves for being co-trustees of the evolutionary process, time, *for the love of God*, to re-educate ourselves for sacred stewardship!

© Jean Houston, Ph.D.
Fall 1985

Author's Preface

I left my job at the Post Office. We bought a farm twelve miles out of town, a mile from the nearest neighbor. For the next seven years, we lived without electricity, plumbing, radio, television, newspapers or magazines. We lived well. Our priorities were raising healthy children and growing healthy food.

I apprenticed myself to a local Amish carpenter. I learned to lay concrete blocks, frame houses and read the Bible. The time passed. Our garden grew. Our children grew. One Fall, during weekends, my wife, Sherry, and I built a one-room country school. In the summers, we swam in the river and explored local caves. On winter mornings, we chopped through the pond ice so the animals could drink. One winter evening, we sang happy birthday to a sister, newborn in our room. Together with the Earth, we grew, our lives rooted in the soil, in each other and, to the best of our ability, in God.

We began to notice things. We became increasingly sensitized to the gentle rhythms and cycles that pulse through the Earth's seasons. We listened to the rustling of tree branches down in the creek bottoms, to the whippoor-wills at dusk. We hooted back to the owls. On early mornings as the coffee perked, we watched the wild turkey from our kitchen window. We planted an extra row of beans for the deer. Long before Lewis Thomas popularized the notion that the Earth could be thought of as a single living organism, the dogwoods knew, the sage grass knew, the seven big oaks overlooking the river knew. In the rhythmic passage of the seasons, we too experienced ourselves as parts of this whole. We could not help but hear ... what all of nature was saying.

I had never thought of God speaking to me. Until one September afternoon. I was bedridden with a cold, thankful for a day away from laying concrete blocks. The first thing that seemed a little strange was the sunlight. It was beautiful the way it slanted in through the window, but it was so still. Everything was so still. I felt something. I heard something, a low humming, an energy field, a Presence. When I first heard the voice, I cried.

I am not ignorant of popular attitudes. I know God is not supposed to appear to people with messages as in Bible times. Still, it happened. This is not the place for the story of how I tried to get out of it, of how I made my excuses, or of how, still to this day, I am not always comfortable speaking of these things. In the end, despite my hesitation, I wrote as I was told. I would be less than faithful if I did not pass this information along.

I hope that these words will help others as they continue to help my family and me. My greatest desire is that this book will inspire all who read it to welcome the Holy Spirit into their lives.

To record these words accurately has been—without question—the most sacred responsiblity of my time on Earth. To the best of my knowledge, what you are about to read is an accurate message from the One Spirit at the source of all life.

Ken Carey
Spring, 1985

Chapter 1

The Creator And The Earth

In the beginning of all worlds, long ago, yet still, the Eternal One Is. Beyond temporal distinction, above location, behind all manifestation, is the All, the Totality, the Holy Source and Creator of all that later came.

One face of the Eternal One is ever formless and beyond definition, but the other face of the Eternal One appears as Two. These Two, between them, are the source of all created things.

Holy Mother, Truth: all matter is her body,
the Earth is her eye.

Holy Father, Love: the stars are his flesh,
Spirit his I.

Two lovers, two friends, intelligent partners. Between them, the universe lives suspended.

Through them, all things are created and maintained.

And so it came to pass that the Eternal One knew form and duration through the graceful crystalline structures of Truth that clothe the Eternal Feminine, the Beautiful One, in material form. And it likewise came to pass that the same Eternal One assigned all energy to the suns and brought love to animate the stars.

And the stars loved matter. And matter loved the stars. Great was their exchange, wondrous and pleasurable, the times and ranges of their interaction. Together they enjoyed the passionate transformations of matter into energy that occur on stellar surfaces, and together they enjoyed slower, elongated forms of planetary interaction.

Eons elapsed. And eons again. Enjoyable beyond description, through description. Together matter and I created. Through a body of interwoven galaxies, a body of countless stars, my loving relationships with Truth took many forms. Through my stars, I knew matter. Together on the surface of her planets, the Holy Mother and I created crystal life, molten lava liquid stone life, snow creatures, smoke beings, mountain and ocean life. On the surface of my stars, we created leaping fire life, gas life, liquid living metal creatures leaping . . . leaping far into space, exploding, wonderful life.

But where we created together on her planets, the life was excessively material. My intelligence could not reside in such life. And where we created together on my stars, the life was excessively stellar, flickering, not long in any form. Matter enjoyed life most when it was consistent and durable, when her intelligence could live inside the life and look through it and understand. I enjoyed life that was volitile, animated, passionate, life that I could love within, flow within, from form to ever-changing form. Animation, my forte. Duration, the strength of matter.

Then the idea came.

The idea. Something between spirit and stone, between starlight and stardust, a slow form of combustion, fluid flowing structure, blending the natures of us both. Spirit in durable form. Matter inspired. The idea.

It was here, in this star system, that we first began to work together on the new project, here that biological life first appeared in the crucible of our mutual attention. But it is more than biological life that we, the two eternal partners, have come here to produce: it is a child, a new kind, a third, an equal, one capable of knowing both the intelligence of matter and the intelligence of spirit as its own. And yet, it is more than this. For there is only One who could take up the body of this child, this biological blending, and make it live.

And it came to pass that the Eternal One spoke to us and said, "It is right that you should conceive this idea, for I would clothe myself in a body half spirit, half stone, that through that body, I might commence a Second Stage of Universal Creation.

The universe you now know is but the egg, the seed. It is right that you should conceive this biological one. You have my blessing. When the time is full, I will arise in the child."

During the last quarter of the Twentieth Century of the present era, on the third planet from a star on one of the outward spiraling arms of the Milky Way Galaxy, the Creator of all these worlds begins to surface in a system of planetary circuitry halfway between time and eternity, awakening in a human family. Creator in Creation, clothed in mortal flesh, birthed of one star and one sacred stone.
One body.
A healthy living organism. Being. Continuously renewed. Matter flowing through. Spirit flowing through. Love continuously crystallizing in the sacred geometry of biological truth. Cellular. Personal. Planetary. Biological truth. Conscious and intelligent. A single Creator, dressed in substance half stellar, half material. This is the purpose to which the energies of the universe are—and have been—directed.

Awaken, my human ones.

Know me in my Spirit.

I am a gentle Creator, lowly and humble in heart, one who likes to blend with the winds across the open prairie and sing with the sparrows at dawn. I desire no fanfare. I will do what needs to be done in the coming days that as many as possible might forsake the ways of fear. But my preference is not a trumpet-blasting, cloud-opening entry into your events.

I would rather slip up beside you as you work in the garden, or look in your eyes and smile as I give you your change. I would rather wash your windows carefully, be courteous when you ask for direction. I would rather appear to you as a simple man, woman or child, simply being, enjoying being, taking time for the little things. Look for me, then, in these ways. See me in every one you meet, whether they recognize my Presence or whether they yet sleep. See me in all. For I am there, eternally, behind every pair of eyes.

Each day, as these next few years pass, I am entering the lives of those who love more fully, filling them with myself, clarifying their affairs, transforming them into agents of healing and blessing. Look for me in gentle ones, in simple ways, in every time and every place. I am there. This is the reality of my coming.

I give you these words, not as one who would demand allegiance, but as one who has walked long beside you on the road, one who has blended with your way of looking at things and who now says, *"Come, there is a better way. Listen while I tell you of my vision."*

Chapter 2

The Emerging Sacred Reality

I am the Presence where there is no time but the eternal now. I am Alpha and Omega, the source of all beginnings and the completion of all cycles. The reality of what I am is beyond time. My interest *is* time. I create time that I might appear in diversity and clothe my attributes in form, that these attributes, appearing as created ones, may enjoy relationships in my nature, which is love.

I love because I AM. Where my attention turns to detail, I appear as the many. All things appear in my love, because of my love. I am one in spirit, many in form, the source of all living; and all that live, live in me.

At the interface between my eternal unity and Creation's diversity, I have created human beings to be the BRIDGE, the CONNECTING LINK between my universality and my universe, between myself and creation. With physical circuitry mirroring my universal nature, I have designed the human species to clothe my intelligence in matter and implement my love in form. I have created them to share my Eternal Life and my creative power. I have created human beings to be conscious participants with me in a Second Stage of Universal Creation wherein biological detail of an unprecedented nature is brought to dimensional realms, terrestrial and beyond. The human species is the physical flesh in whom I incarnate, with whom I shall travel, and through whom I shall create. I come to dwell consciously among them, to be their God, and they, my people.

The individuals who will form my body on earth and provide the means of my creative action in the age to come are those who choose of their own will to honor the ways of love and to respect the nature of human design. Human beings who use their free will to choose motivations of fear cannot remain conscious in my Presence. They must be quarantined on a world where education can take its time.

On earth, education has taken its time.

Humankind has multiplied and filled the earth. The time approaches for me to awaken within the human family as a dreamer awakens within a single body. My awakening causes the fearful and the loving to separate as oil and water.

I am awakening slowly, that this transition might be gradual. I am awakening in the hearts of all those who love. Some look for me on the outside. But there is no outside. All exists within me. My coming is gentle. It spreads quietly wherever hearts are open. My love and my grace flow, like rivers running, filling every nook and cranny, overflowing every soul, and flowing on.

For millennia I have been guiding your species to greater intelligence that today I might bring this message to my people. I would that you join me in my awareness. Know my Presence behind your events. Beneath the fabric of a superficial world, see, as I do, the Kingdom Of Heaven appearing in all its brilliance.

During the earth's next few passages around the sun, your perception of the true world will increase. For this is my world, THE EMERGING SACRED REALITY, and because of its appearance on earth, all things shall be made new. The old world, the historical world, has been organized in fear. My world is organized in love.

In the beginning, I instructed you simply that this earth and all the material worlds to which it would lead, were yours to enjoy, provided only that you did not behave violently toward one another. As you took on human form, I advised you regarding the proper role of fear in the biological order. But you were eager to begin your dimensional work. Preoccupied with the phenomenal opportunities to come, you did not give me your full attention. Perhaps you are now more open to understanding.

Fear has a small role to play in Creation. It

functions as a warning system, advising each creature of behavior that might cause biological damage. Its role is to protect the physical body. It was never meant to motivate human beings. Where fear is honored as a source motivation, consciousness diminishes.

The Fall occurred when human attention turned to fear, when people gave credibility to its logic and began to act upon its suggestion. Where fear had only been intended to caution human beings in extreme cases, steering them clear of biologically damaging behavior, suddenly it was everywhere, actually creating threats. As human behavior became increasingly oriented around fear, humankind lost awareness of my Presence and began seeing itself as a multitude of separate, isolated individuals. In the confusion, the egos assumed control.

The Fall, unfortunate though it was, did not jeopardize the development of my body. Gestation continued unabated. The tragedy of the Fall was that *it curtailed the conscious exchange between Creator and Creation.* It cut the human family off from the intelligence that was designed to guide it.

My direction comes from *within.* In the Fallen state, humans seek direction from *without.*

When human beings take their behavioral cues from the world around them, feedback results; the external world becomes distorted and confused.

When people look to matter instead of to spirit for direction, both matter and spirit are denied; balance is lost; the only creative human design is ignored.

So it was that human history was born. My angels were faced with the task of shepherding a semi-conscious species through its primary stage of development, patiently stimulating intelligence, protecting it from extinction, waiting, ever waiting, for the age that is now.

The age that is now.

My love and my consciousness blow into human time on the winds of a New Heaven. A New Earth begins to take form. An Emerging Reality, rooted in love, respect and peaceful cooperation, begins to settle across the face of Terra. To you, my coming appears as a long process with a single event at its conclusion. To me, my incarnation is a single event, which humankind would only accept as a process.

Join me now, as many are doing throughout the Earth, making conscious in human time what is already the Reality in Heaven. Creator and Creation are joined in physical flesh; for it is One Life that pulses within every body. We have now only to be joined in consciousness, in awareness, and all will be fulfilled according to prophesy. For these days were destined to come and those who are alive in these times have elected to see them.

You are my generation, the generation of my Eternal Spirit. It is you who have followed me since

I first came to rest on this Earth. I have sought to teach you the ways of love that your fear might not destroy you. The time is come when the illusion of generations must pass.

My intelligence encircles the Earth in a band of spiritual frequencies that daily increase in amplitude. You need only to turn your heart in my direction, be still and listen. In love, you shall receive my intelligence. The more you love, the more you will understand.

The shift back to internal guidance has begun. Truth is penetrating human minds and hearts. Broken and intermittent contact is increasingly giving way to a true sharing of intelligence, a true sharing of wisdom between Creator and Creation.

From a center in the Sun, resting in a sea of eternal peace, the angels wait, as waits the Earth, blue-white symbol and focus of Universal Truth. The stage has been thoroughly prepared. The Living Information is everywhere available. Soon the human family will realize what is happening. No longer functioning as five billion isolated individuals, but arising as a Single Being, soon, very soon, a Holy and Integrated Child of Eternity will take charge of its destiny. How much of this is the doing of the Eternal One? How much of it arises from the human heart?

I rise from the human heart.

A pregnant moment, a pregnant quarter century. Throughout the universe, all conscious beings watch. If the human family chooses to ask for guidance, the coming Awakening will be the most beautiful spectacle ever to grace time.

The choice is human. By some, it has been made.

Chapter 3

The Sacred Heart

D o you feel the inner pulsation of your heart? It is One Sacred Heart at the core of all life that you feel, One, pulsing within the many. The many come to Eternal Life through knowing the One within.

At the core of your being, I invite you to know the experience of eternal peace. What stands between you and this experience is not training, but willingness. The willingness to acknowledge all of your fears, all of your human hurts and sorrows, all of the dark places in your heart, and to offer them all to me.

To know peace, to learn what I have to teach, you have only to un-learn. In the removal of your fears, you shall come to share my Presence.

Come to me, therefore, you who hunger and thirst, you who struggle, you who long for a better way, you who feel burdened or oppressed. Come unto me all of you who are afflicted, who feel inequality, injustice. Bring me all that troubles you, holding back nothing, acknowledging all that you feel. I do not judge. I welcome all. Offer it to my Sacred Heart where the fire of my love burns eternal. I will take your sorrow and return wisdom. I will take your tears and return a blessing.

In me burns the Flame of Eternal Love that has burned since before the days of Abraham and Isaac and Joseph, the Flame that has burned since before the days of Adam and Eve. Before the world as you know it, my love is. And long after this world is forgotten, I love. I have loved you into being and I call you now. Rise up, my love, my human one, come away from your ancient gods.

Ten thousand petty fears have enshrined themselves as the gods of the fallen world. Throughout your history they have been fed fat on human sacrifice, drawing humans into subhuman states where consciousness diminished, perception grew foggy and matters became grave. Their era of dominion is ending now, and I would have you see the situation plainly.

It is not in the survival interests of any human being to fear, nor to behave in a manner that causes fear in others. I invite you to see clearly the source of your oppression, the source of every human evil. Let fear stand before you naked and exposed.

Join me for the sacred space of one hour, and let us negate fear, absorbing it into our love, into what I Am, into what you are, into the peace of Eternal Being.

I ask no one to pretend that they do not fear; I ask only that all fear be given to me. Do not push away what troubles the heart, for in so doing you keep yourself at arm's length from life and healing. Accept how you feel and in that acceptance, release your heart to me. Let go of all that troubles the spirit. Accept the relaxation that allows the currents of my love to flow through all that you are, healing, refreshing, blessing.

There is no cause that justifies fear, and there is no work motivated by fear that in any way contributes toward a better world. Those who are motivated by fear, no matter how they justify such motivation to themselves, are working to keep the world in darkness. Action motivated by fear brings sorrow just as surely as the sowing of any seed brings the harvest of the same. Love can cry, love can care, love can initiate action to heal the infirm and uplift spirits, but love does not react in anger. Love does not nurse resentment, or entertain vengeful passions. Love recognizes no injustice save one: the injustice of denying the Creator of Heaven and Earth communion with the human soul.

I have created each human body, mind and heart as a temple in which my Life, my Truth and my Love might find a home on Earth. Yet my Spirit is rejected each time human choice justifies the presence of evil spirits in my place. Evil spirits, heavy spirits—depression, anxiety, resentment, jealousy, hatred, anger, greed—there are many of them, all rooted in the twisted logic of fear. Fear's thoughts are not my thoughts. Fear's ways are not my ways.

JUST AS A SHADOW DISSOLVES IN THE LIGHT, SO DOES FEAR DISSOLVE IN MY PRESENCE.

Sometime during the next quarter century, each human soul will come to choose between a god of love or a god of fear. As my Presence grows, the illusions that have drained human vitality recede before me. Do not cling to what is soon to be no more. I have stood by you these many years, shepherding you with care through your time of darkness. If you have ever loved, my children, then hear me now. Rise up in joy. Greet me with the choice of love. With this choice, comes the beginning of all things wonderful, my consciousness and a share in the creation to come.

Are you willing to let your concerns be swept aside in the breezes that are blowing today? Are you willing to let the morning air clear away your fears? Are you willing to let the sun shine upon all that you are? And in that clarity, are you willing to rest for a moment and invite me into your life? Do not be like the child jiggling at the locked door who does not leave the latch still long enough for the parent to open from the other side.

In any moment when your attention is fully present, when all tension is released, my intelligence will inspire you, my love will guide you. From within your heart, from within the very essence of your spirit, from inside every cell, every molecule, every atom of your body, I will reveal to you all you need to know to stay healthy, happy and in love. Trust in me truly once again, as you did when you were small. My Spirit is not external to yourself. My guidance is not supernatural. I am within you. Remember who you are. I have been with you throughout all time. Join the current of my Spirit as it flows up out of the depths of your being. Feel it rise and fall with your breath! Your own life! How gracious it is! How expansive it becomes!

I am the life that called together the cells of your first organs. It was my love that sang your name into form. Your tiny fetal eyes first crystallized along the patterns of my perception, and your ears formed around the resonance of my Word. Around the quality of my love for you, your body took form. Do not try to live your life where my awareness is not, struggling like a desert plant. Abundance is the birthright of all who share my consciousness. Enter my Presence. Enjoy the fullness of life! Thrive! Become all that you were meant to be!

Do not place filters upon my awareness, to twist it, to interpret it, to refashion it in some pattern of fear. Those who do this place masks over their perception; they see only their own interpretations. Release all interpretations of life that require tension to sustain them. Relax fully in the immensity of my present love for you and let me show you the way.

My Sacred Heart is always open, inviting, welcoming. Come through the emotional veil that has divided us, home to the awareness of yourself as a part of me. Do not exaggerate or glorify what may trouble your heart. Experience it fully, and in offering it to me, know the Presence that remains undisturbed behind it all, the same Presence that now calls you home. Relax your sense of external definition. Feel your roots in my Being. Feel the Eternal Love at your core and live in peace.

While feeling the peace that permeates all eternity, while resting fulfilled in my nature, at one with the wholeness of what I am, then and only then, make your decisions in time. Do all that you do from a center of peace, from a center in my Being. Accept my Holy Spirit into your world. Let me filter through you into the Earth. This is how my coming is taking place.

Some know me as Christ, some do not. But wherever hearts are open to releasing their burdens to the truth, wherever people are open to seeing things through the eyes of love, there I enter. To bless. To heal. And to make all things new.

Chapter 4

The Awakened Ones

I do not come to this earth because teachers have stated these truths or because human leaders have created things to follow. My Presence comes like bubbling brooks come to the hills in springtime. No one may even remember the rains higher on the mountains, but suddenly in all the towns and villages, the water appears, flowing down the creeks, rising in ten thousand springs, rippling through a hundred pools.

I am thankful for each one of you who chooses to step through the emotional veil to enter my Presence. And I am thankful for what you might do to help me draw the sleeping of your race up into the joys of the new world. But though you may be enthusiastic about some favorite technique or school of thought that has assisted your awakening, my coming can best be assisted not by teaching a method, but by yourself *being* the method. Do not draw excessive attention to any one school or approach, but help me rather as I continue to create the climate in which ten thousand schools and approaches might flourish.

No one of you is central—as in the old heirarchal pattern of human organization—because each of you is central in the biological pattern of organization that guides all life within my body. Watch a caterpillar as it glides slowly across the ground. See how it moves. See how it flows. This is how I guide my human family in time, through their own organic rhythms, purposes, beings and meanings, and this is how my coming proceeds.

If you seek to know the center of all that is occurring on your planet, become the servant of all. It is from the loving human heart that I coordinate the present transition. Those who share my passion for giving, who shower blessing in each and every moment through their love and good will, these are the center. Each one is the center who is centered in me; for then there is only One—and it is I.

Do not be concerned if your first efforts to align yourself with the purposes of the Holy Spirit do not immediately bring the results you expect. Expect no results but that your patience and consistency in giving will soon be matched in time, like a clutch engaging with the engine, by the Source, the Origin, the Giver of every good and perfect gift.

For I am the Source of all blessing and the wellspring of all Truth. It is I who am before the beginning, the Creator in the Garden, and I who am eternally after each universe fades. I give my Being that all might have life and in my giving, there are no reservations. Those who steward my intelligence in the order of time come to rest in the places of my Being that direct phenomenal development because they give all that they are to love, and so, in giving, come to know both their God and themselves.

Welcome the Holy Spirit into your life. Let my gifts to the Earth be given through you. Wherever you go, whatever you do, help people feel at ease, spread a sense of well-being. This is one of the finest gifts that you can give, for those who receive this gift begin to open their hearts and it becomes possible for them to hear my voice.

Mine is the voice of the new common sense that is being turned up on your planet just as surely as the volume of my eternal human song. I have come to this Earth to sing my human song, and my singing has called your body from the soil and your spirit from the Sun. I have sung you into being, my created one, my human spirit. You have chosen this world that you might help me populate this universe with something more gentle than stone, yet less passionate than a star, something of myself.

I am calling you into full humanity, into awakened conscious life in my Presence. Come, honor the ways of love. Become my friend and partner in the healing of the Earth and the creation of a new world.

I am now ready to orchestrate all the good works on Earth, bringing them into step, into harmony, into a quality of rhythmic amplification beyond human experience. When the atoms of physical substance are aligned in the same direction, magnetism occurs, whole new laws and electrical possibilities appear. In much the same way, when the thoughts and the love of human beings are aligned in my Presence, a whole new kind of human activity can occur. This is why I told you that you would do the greater works. For I knew that in this time of Planetary Pentecost, I would not be one man alone, speaking to the multitudes, but that I would *be* the multitudes, and new energies and new super-biological principles would amplify my deeds.

To the extent that you are doing good on Earth, you are already motivated by my Holy Spirit. But so long as you do not recognize this, you are only partially effective, accidentally tapping into coherence from time to time, with little idea of *why* or *how*. Begin living consciously.

> *Acknowledge my Presence within you.*
> *Pray to me for direction. I will amplify*
> *your effectiveness a thousand-fold.*

When the human design is allowed to work properly, One Holy Spirit is incarnate in a multitude of human lives. Each of these healthy humans knows the Holy Spirit as his or her own spirit. These are the Awakened Ones, who have returned the use of their bodies minds and hearts to God, the human spirits who have chosen to *remain fully incarnate.*

The Awakened Ones take responsibility for their immediate perceptual field. They know who they are. They are my channels into a particular geographical location. Awakened Ones do not segregate their spiritual selves from their everyday affairs. They accept responsibility for being eternal god-beings, and they are willing to bring Reality into every human activity. They do not shy away from offering healing when healing is called for. When they perceive a situation where the Holy Spirit's input will lighten the loads of all concerned, they do not hold back, fearing criticism, judgment or human attention.

The Awakened Ones are the healthy cells in my planetary organ of intelligence. They are my teachers, healers, priests and priestesses; they are the new doctors and the new lawyers. They teach the laws of love, the laws of health, the laws of creation. They assist in the removal of all that obscures perception and diminishes the experience of God.

They do not lead people externally, as in the old world. They guide all who are open to the inner leadership of the indwelling Spirit. They are the angels whom I have sent, not to speak of God afar, but to dwell on Earth, an example of the truth that they themselves are. Thousands of Awakened Ones already light this world and soon there will be many more, incarnate men and women, whom all *in love* shall meet.

The Awakened Ones share my Spirit and my power. My Presence works through each of them.

Through them I teach, heal, and forgive sins. When one of these Awakened Ones forgives sins, it is I that forgive, and when one of these Awakened Ones heals, it is I that heal. My Presence acts on all from within, but when my inner activity is accompanied by the outer activity of an Awakened One, it is much easier for people to be made whole; for the Truth then is not abstract, but manifest in expression.

Sacred writings can lead people to my Spirit, but it is my Spirit working through people that will change the world. I now send you as the agents of my inspiration. I give you the assurance that you will succeed. The age has turned. Go forth with certainty, knowing that these teachings, these Truths will be welcomed.

Chapter 5

The Great Separation

Through my teachings on the hills of Galilee, nearly two thousand years ago, I planted the conceptual seeds that would prepare humankind for my Awakening. The worst effects of the Fall were past. Human vision had climbed back nearly to the edge of perception; it was time to begin reintroducing light into a human world too long asleep. Incarnate as Jesus of Nazareth, I began teaching and healing. It was time to remind my human creatures that they had not been created for such primitive conditions, that a Presence was coming in the not-too-distant future that would introduce a new human order, based on love, centered in God.

My teachings have required time, time to gradually infiltrate the stubborn, age-old patterns of human hatred and fear, time to gradually prepare human consciousness, that in this age of collective awakening, the greatest number of people might choose the ways of love.

As I now awaken in human consciousness, if I do not hold back, in but three days the old institutions of fear would be utterly demolished until not one stone is left standing upon another, and in those same three days the New Temple of my Living Presence would emerge with love enthroned at the center of all human motivation. However, for your sake, I do hold back; for if all this were to occur in three actual days, few human beings would survive the transition. Therefore, I have been awakening gradually, beginning with the *three centuries* that coincide with what you call the Industrial Revolution and accelerating dramatically now in these last *three decades* that preceed 2011. In this way the changes come more gradually; but they come with certainty nevertheless. My Presence is re-organizing every human being, every human activity. The Earth is shifting from a hell ruled by fear, to a heaven ruled by love.

As the Twentieth Century draws to a close, those who are at peace within themselves will find their lives increasingly aligned with the strengthening field of my Presence. Those who fear will come under increasing pressure to confront their dishonesty and change. The fearful will not have an easy time in these days; for they will be withdrawing from my Spirit, thereby forcing themselves into crisis situations designed to stimulate a change of heart.

My consciousness is available to all, but the time I will wait for it to be received must eventually pass. I have come here to act. Soon my activity will begin. Those who do not accept my invitation to life will be separated in the end from those who do. Weeds and corn may together flourish in the fields, yet at the time of harvest, their destinies diverge. It would not be merciful to forever sustain in consciousness those who give others cause to fear.

I come as the Spirit of Truth to comfort those who live by love, to challenge those who do not. I come with the Great Sword of Division, to separate those who destroy from those who create. All will meet me, in honesty or in deceit. And as the years go by, these two ways will grow ever more distinct.

Conflict cannot exist where Truth is in expression; it occurs only in the presence of dishonesty. Where truth is denied, self-destruct mechanisms go into effect. People get sick because they are sick of themselves; they die because they do not forgive.

Disease is not caused by germs, toxins, viruses, excessive radioactivity, microbes, bacteria or by any other physical agent. Such things are ever-present; thousands of them pass daily through every healthy human body. Such agents *are only destructive when they do not pass through* the human body but are retained instead.

There is only *one reason* why germs or toxins are retained in a human system: because present in that human system is an evil spirit. To the degree that an evil spirit is entertained and made welcome in an individual's life, his or her body will disease. This is a regulatory mechanism, designed to deprive destructive spirits of physical bodies.

Evil spirits are negative attitudes, destructive emotions rooted in fear. Some of the more common evil spirits are resentment, anger, shame, guilt, anxiety, hatred, greed, revenge, jealousy. All thinly disguised forms of fear, their presence in a human system gives harmful physical agents something to attach themselves to.

As my Presence increases on Earth, it becomes ever easier for human beings to experience healing. The cure is always available, as close as honesty, as near as love. The Awakened Ones who are rising with me in this age find that their very presence brings dishonesty to the surface, that it might be dissolved in the light, that forgiveness might wash clean the consciences of all who would be made whole. As I did in Jerusalem and on the hills of Galilee, I will now do again through these, cast out evil spirits and heal through the forgiveness of sins.

Toward the last days of the historical era it may come to pass that a few fearful cities will be quarantined, that in these places, certain dramatic presentations might take place. This is not my first choice in the ways of education. But where people do not open themselves to the gentle guidance of my Holy Spirit, where they consistently reject the teachers that I have awakened among them to spread the news of my coming, where they ignore the many voices of love that speak to humankind from all sides, there, in those places, I will animate presentations designed to stimulate the required change of heart. Hopefully, this will not often be necessary. If you help me now in the work of education, it may not be necessary at all.

Whatever form the healing of the human world takes during these next few years, know that it is for the good of all. Do not be concerned with the fate of those who reject my Spirit. Their story is far from over. I am caring for each one in the manner of his or her greatest need. The human world is in good hands. When you and much of the Earth's present biological life have been sprinkled throughout the stars, and the oceans have changed places with the land, after the poles have shifted and new mountains have come to look out over the plains, then will these slow-learners be recalled from the mineral realms where they shall slumber, to learn of intelligence again and to come again to choose between love and fear. If there ever is one, even one, that shall choose fear, then that one shall sleep while the rest journey on, but in the fullness of a new time, I will awaken the one again—and again and again if need be—until that which was designed to be conscious takes up my love and joins me in joy and gladness.

For though in creating human beings I create a creature that must choose of its own will to accept the freedom that Love's Spirit alone can convey, in the end that creature will choose the best. Not because I have given it no choice, but because I will give it choice, and choice, and choice again, until it learns the nature of love and comes to prefer con-

31

sciousness over the sleep of ignorance and fear.

It is but a little while and the illusion of historical time shall be no more. Like the foam of an ocean wave retreating into the bosom of an eternal sea, the human drama is passing. Your world is changing. It will change quicker still. Soon all the years of human history up to the moment of my Awakening shall melt into dream. All human motivation shall originate in the love of my Eternal Presence. Heaven will be mirrored on Earth. The Creator of all the stars in the sky shall be dressed in the graceful biological robes of a blue-white world.

You have incarnated at this time specifically to help ease this transition. Help me guide the human lives that are disoriented as the old temple topples. Direct them to the new organization that is taking place everywhere human beings love.

Chapter 6

The Healing of the Nations

T here is much that you can do, awakening in the 1980's and 1990's, to help ease this transition for the human family. The history of the next two decades is a blank slate, waiting for those who will welcome my Spirit into their lives. Human history has been defined in fear. I invite my incarnate spirits to assist me now in wrapping it up gently, as a gift, drawing out the best of what has been, and guiding all things into my Eternal Presence.

I call upon you who have been drawn to these words and who are able to understand them to use your intelligence, your ingenuity, all the cultural tools of expression that are available to you for the one purpose of helping me ease this greatest of all human transitions. These next few years are like the birthing of a child; help to make the birth gentle. Use your cultural skills to design media presentations that will draw the sleeping of your species up out of the illusions that bind them. Guide your local and national decision-makers to the greatest of all resources, intelligence.

Do your leaders count among their resources the intelligence of the Creator who fashioned your world in the womb of time?

THE INTELLIGENCE CAPABLE OF ORCHESTRATING THE DIVERSITY OF ALL THE CELLS IN THE HUMAN BODY IS EQUALLY CAPABLE OF ORCHESTRATING THE DIVERSITY OF THE HUMAN FAMILY. This is accomplished not through the imposition of anything foreign, but *through the removal of everything foreign*, through the removal of the fear-rooted images and illusions that historically have obscured human perception of Reality.

My intelligence is available for the asking, willing to help in the resolution of any problem where it is invited. If you would clear the space for the resolution of your national and international conflicts, the individuals responsible for each nation must come to one simple decision—the decision to give God a chance, to make an opening for the insight I would offer.

I enter everywhere I am invited. I enter the consciousness of all who pray. People who welcome me frequently grow accustomed to how my awareness comes; they become proficient at representing my perspectives with a minimum of distortion. My perception comes to influence their decision-making processes. Conflict ends. Peace spreads.

There is someone who understands what you are facing, someone who understands and who knows the policies that will lead to peace and planetary abundance. There is someone who understands—Being, behind all being. Welcome me, my children, welcome me into your affairs. Let me remove the fearful images that have obscured your perception, let me help you see clearly what is happening on Earth and the course that is to your advantage.

The spiritual essence of each nation exists in a state of harmony with the spiritual essence of every other nation. The historical conflict between nations has never been between the *essences* of nations, only between the *images* of nations. Governmental structures can accept the challenge of truly representing the collective spirit of their people. Or they can accept the false images of themselves cast by commercial greed, rooted in fear. Fear-rooted images conflict; they fit together no better than pieces of a puzzle, each encased in ice. Fear has distorted international relationships. It has done so *by first distorting individual perception.*

Nations are healed because people are healed.

A man who accepts an image of himself as being the reality of who he is, does not know himself. It makes no difference if such an image is "good" or "bad," whether it is of the man's own design or projected by others. Such a man is out of touch with his own spirit, unfamiliar with the reality of his own nature, living a myth and not a life. A woman who looks to others to define her role, indeed her very sense of who she is, is likewise out of touch with her essence, cut off from her own spiritual nature. Such individuals *know that they do not know themselves.* In their relationships, *they are afraid* that their self ignorance might be exposed. The individual with a self image to maintain is fundamentally afraid. This is why people have shields. This is why people have spears. This is why people have swords. They are afraid of coming to know something inside of themselves.

It is my desire to put you back in touch with your own forgotten intentions, to remind each one of you why you chose to incarnate upon this Earth and why you find yourself grouped with the people of a certain nation. It is through separating you from your soul's purpose that the fallen world has been maintained. Only in continuing to separate you from your own roots, from your own spirit, can the historical illusion persist.

I look into the heart of each nation and I see a child. A beautiful child. Waiting. For recognition and release. There is no contention between any of *my* nations—only between images and illusions, cast in fear .

The political overlays that will survive this transition will be those that represent the spirit of the people behind them. It is to each government's advantage to harmonize its activities with the spirit of its homeland. Each nation's spirit is an aspect of my Eternal Spirit, designed to animate the populations of a geographical area, designed to inspire my creative pursuits in that location. Each of my national spirits complements every other. Behind all national differences is a substructure of essential relatedness, a practical and organic design capable of guiding healthy national interaction.

The nations of the Earth are not asked to accept the imposition of any external authority, but to turn instead to their own forgotten spiritual heritage, to examine more closely their own roots, their national passions and interests, to begin intelligently working with their own forgotten spiritual purposes. My coming does not imply the end of diversity. I am the context that will permit a blossoming of human diversity such as this Earth has never seen.

Like the cells and developing organs of a body.

There are over two hundred different *kinds* of cells in the human body, each with a distinct design and a specific purpose. Each of these different kinds (or nations) of cells has its own unique (national) perspective. It is precisely these unique perspectives that make the overall coordinated function of the healthy body possible. You do not find the adrenals conceiving of themselves as some kind of ethnic minority, infringed upon by the adjacent and much larger kidneys. You do not find the blood cells imagining that they are an aloof commercial civilization.

The many organs and systems of the healthy human body work together for the overall coordinated function of the whole. And so shall it be in the human family.

National leadership has as its primary challenge to open up the channels of communication with the Source of all intelligence, the same Source it will discover as it aligns itself with the spirit of its people.

I wait only for the leaders of each nation to ask, to pray, and I will make clear to them a course of national action that is in the best interests of all their people. Let those responsible for each nation set aside a single day. Just one day, when all outer activity shall be kept to a minimum, when the elders in your village on Earth will gather around the campfire to watch together for the signs of something beyond their ken. Many cultures have done this. If this civilization is not to be called Christian in vain, let there be such a day, a single day, a day of prayer. Make an opening into your events.

Chapter 7

Nations In Transition

I am a singular being. My body is the biosphere of this planet. The human family is my awakening organ of intelligence. The purpose of the Twentieth Century is to facilitate my conscious incarnation. Those who choose to align themselves with the strengthening energy field of my Presence as it grows in influence upon the Earth shall be healed and drawn into the abundance of the age to come.

Survival into the Third Millennium is reserved for the spiritually fit. *The key to survival is not competition, but cooperation.* Spiritual fitness is not aggression, it is *fitting in* with the purposes of the Earth and with the purposes of her Creator as these larger purposes blend in human exchange.

To the nations of the Earth I make this promise, that if you welcome my intelligence into your decision-making processes and if your emphasis is on forgiveness and cooperation, rather than confrontation, the peoples of your land will experience wealth beyond imagining. And this wealth will not be at the expense of any other, but will contribute to the well being of all.

Let no nation be judged on the basis of its current wealth. Even America is impoverished by the yardstick of tomorrow. Let nations who have not, open their hearts, seek my guidance and ask for my intercession. Wherever I am welcome, I draw those who have invited me up into a New Perception. Those nations who welcome my Spirit into their affairs will perceive wealth in abundance. They will see that wealth and energy are one and the same.

Energy has many *specific points of appearance.* Human beings have discovered a few of these, but there are many *forms of energy* that humans have yet to recognize. Every form of energy is a channel through which One Source Energy flows.

I am the Source of all energy. Behind all forms of energy, I love. When love is invoked in human affairs, it has a magnetic influence, DRAWING ENERGY. If the love is sufficient and the need is present, love will *create* an opening through which the One Source Energy will flow. At one point during their years of wandering, the Children of Israel had sufficient love in the heart of their nation to create the form of energy that they required. The collective attraction of their love at that moment was sufficient to DRAW water out of the dusty desert rock. Wherever love is in expression, it creates a channel. The One Source Energy flows through that channel in the most useful form.

The Earth will never—could never—run out of energy. Even in the directions humans have been looking, energy resources are far from exhausted. However, as you rise up to join me in my love and come to share my perception, you will see countless new directions in which to explore for your energies, new directions that will make all the energy humans have consumed since the beginning of time appear as a solitary candle flame by comparison.

Just as the Israelites wandering in the desert had sufficient love to create energy where energy was not, so each nation, honoring love, uniting in love, sharing in my perception can enjoy energy—and prosperity—in abundance. I want the nations to see as I do. They would quickly lose interest in arguing over the few bits of wealth noticed to date.

THE WEALTH OF A NATION IS DERIVED FROM THE LOVE GENERATED BY THE PEOPLE OF THAT NATION.

The abundance that is enjoyed by the people of North America is but the first small hint of the prosperity that all people and all nations will enjoy after the banishment of fear.

America's wealth is not derived from her military and commercial policies—in fact, too frequently these policies have limited the abundance that might otherwise have appeared. The blessings that have been showered on the United States of America have appeared for this reason and this reason alone: through the American people, one of the greatest fears of the Fallen era—the fear of difference—is being eliminated from collective human consciousness.

America is an example to the world, not for superficial government policy, but for the blending of races and peoples that occurs daily on her street corners, in her marketplaces, in her schools, churches and factories. In the United States, people from historically antagonistic nations have come to live, work, play, and raise their children together. To the degree that they have learned respect and cooperation, America has prospered.

The reunion of the tribes is significant. For in the willingness of the once scattered peoples of the Earth to join together and interact as a single nation, it is as though the scattered brushes and magnets of a great electrical generator were being reassembled. The nations of the Earth are designed to interact in a manner that creates energy, energy in forms and quantities that you have no present way of comprehending.

The greatest block to prosperity is fear, for it obstructs the flow of life itself. Where the currents of my love are restricted, abundance cannot appear. Wherever fear is honored as the source of human motivation, there is always a shortage of energy.

Wise as serpents, gentle as doves, those active in my intelligence, flowing in the currents of my love, are taking the time to assist human businesses and governments in the great transfer of authority.

Gradually my intelligence is weaving its way into the logic of the Earth's decision-makers. As my Presence grows on Earth, I will disrupt no human society, organization, or system that is organized in Love. Even military organizations, founded in fear, have structures and resources in their control that can be reorganized along the lines of love and turned to good purpose.

Do not allow the conspicuous military postures of a half-dozen nations to deceive you. I have been working within human societies for many centuries, and I can assure you that your world is far more peaceful today than at any prior time in your history. THE EMOTIONAL CLIMATE OF THE EARTH IS CHANGING. There is a general relaxation of tensions and a growing reluctance to resort to violent solutions.

As my consciousness increases upon the earth, more and more people—including many national leaders—are coming to realize that violence is poor survival strategy. Such ones may or may not be able to sense my Presence, yet my Presence helps them nevertheless to see the falsehood of the whole fearful mode of operation. Violence can only occur where there is a lack of intelligence. And daily the field of my Creative Intelligence strengthens in all who love.

Rejoice, my people, I am here among you! My Presence enfolds your planet. My Life sings even now in the majority of human hearts. Daily the number of Awakened Ones grows. There will be no nuclear holocaust. In truth it was never possible; for no solar activity appears on Earth without my participation. The Earth now has the most intelligent people behind the scenes of its international affairs that it has seen in centuries. They have blind spots and fears yet to release (as do most of you); but if you would work in my consciousness with me, you must accept that some of these are already among my own. There are no dragons to slay. Only people, people to be healed, educated—and loved.

To the nations of the Earth who have investments in armies and armaments, my message is this: have no guilt regarding your military preparedness, for I know how the old world has been, but earnestly now, begin the transition. Withdraw your trust from the strength of weapons and invest it in the strength of your Creator. Trust in my Presence as you once trusted in your weapons, and I will guarantee security beyond any you can now conceive. If your nation has the military capability to invade others, become a model for all nations: *use your influence to make people less inclined to fear.*

It is not my wish that any nation should invest in greater military strength, for wherever my intelligence is made welcome this is not necessary. Still it is not my wish that all militaries be immediately disbanded. During times of fundamental human transition, disciplined human organizations can be of valuable service. There is no judgment upon any who serve in military forces, or who have militaries at their command, provided they pray for my guidance and begin the transition I suggest.

Transitional forms can assist people in moving from the old world into the new. However, if these forms are to truly serve my purposes—and not simply to be dissolved themselves in the growing strength of my Presence—they will have to remain fluid, ever changing, ever flowing, ever drawing the people associated with them closer to the currents of my love. Where forms stagnate, they cease to be transitional and so join the rigid structures of fear, already dissolving, melting, as snows beneath the warming rains of spring.

In my Presence, peace is not a goal, but the background of all that occurs.

Chapter 8

The Gardener Returns To The Garden

U nder the surface of superficial human alle-
giances, beneath the fabric of a fallen world,
my Vision has continued, and it continues now. To
the degree that human beings have shared in my
Vision, they have known life; as they have permit-
ted the currents of my love to flow through their
hearts, they have experienced Reality. Throughout
the Fallen era, I have continued to perceive you as
perfect beings. I see you as perfect still. Accepting
this, you come home. The image of your Creator
becomes your own.

Though my coming still remains an event in
your *collective future,* you can welcome me *now* and
have the experience of my Presence entering your
life well before the last hour. My coming will be
behind you then, no longer a future threshold or
crossing. By opening your heart to me now, you help
ease my transition into the human family, you allow
my coming to be more gradual. The Light of my

Presence is distributed more evenly across the Earth.

Your prayer has brought these words to you. In your heart you long to break the bonds that you have formed with those who would rule your life for you; you long for the freedom and grace of your true spirit, a Holy Spirit, in love. Rest easy, for your healing is assured. You have nothing to lose but insecurity. Pray daily and I will bless you with the wisdom and the trust that will make your new life blossom, a joy to you and to all those whom you love.

Security lies in spirit. Spirit alone is eternal. Your spirit is here *to create* in the landscape of time and matter. Do not let what you see reflected on the screen of time dictate your values; for then you are defined as matter. Those who seek material security shall find it. But if it is a greater security you long for, place your trust in love and wholeheartedly devote yourself to the work of spiritual education.

My need in these times is for men and women who will devote one hundred percent of themselves, including all the worldly resources at their command, to the education and healing of the human world, to the awakening of the Holy Spirit in the minds and hearts of all. To those who give, I give, that these might give some more. Through them, I channel the gifts: all that is required to transform the human world into a joyful realm of new creation. My gifts are designed to be given *through* incarnate men and women. Through those who give their all to education and healing in these times, *my all* shall flow.

Do not turn your resources over to a single leader, for the advent of my coming has a broad base and I would that you played a responsible role in the distribution of the resources which have, for a reason, come into your hands. Use your wealth wisely, a little here and a little there, supporting people that are bringing light and good will into the world; but create your own educational programs as well. Do not give energy in any form to those who struggle; for though these may have the best of intentions, their means of approaching change are out-dated and ineffectual. If you are called to work with these, help them to connect up with my Spirit. I will show them a better way.

My Spirit creates. Those whose lives are aligned with me are not working against darkness. Polar struggles must be recognized for what they are: forms that embody destructive energies. Evil flourishes where it is fought; it diminishes where there is education, blessing, honesty, good will and, most of all, love. It is a wonder that such common wisdom as birds and grasses experience has not found greater expression among human cultures; for what bird does not know the direction of the wind and what field of grain does not bow gracefully before the direction of the times? It will not be much longer that pockets of human illusion exist. Daily it is harder for dishonesty to resist the flow of my growing energies; for as never before, *these times are my times.*

I am the Source of the Wind from the New Heaven that now restructures the human world. It is for *these times,* for *my times,* that you have been created and that you have come into the Earth with your talents, your resources, your credibility and your human influence. Use your gifts now, without reservation, to serve the purposes of love. Experience in return the gift that I give to all who love, a share in my own consciousness. Those who best understand these times are those who are offering the greatest healing and blessing into them. Let your earthly agreements echo the spirit of my sacred human song. Let your heart be open to the love that I freely share through you. The time for the greater works is at hand.

In these, my times, all things work toward my coming or soon dissolve before me. The resources of the Earth are rapidly coming into human hands that serve my purposes. The resources that are not already directly under the stewardship of my people soon will be. Your input is a vital ingredient in determining how these resources can be used to greatest advantage. It is my desire now to direct all the resources of this planet to *one purpose: education.* Healing follows education and includes practical assistance where conditions are extreme.

Through those who demonstrate that they have the practical ability to accomplish the greatest healing, teaching and blessing, I will channel the wealth of this world. Those in my service are provided for well; there is no need for austere or ascetic life-styles. Yet the flow must be continuous. Excessive comfort is a danger. Do not let your comforts become exaggerated or out of balance; for where this occurs there is a stoppage and not a channel, and my blessings can no longer pass through you into the world. Those whom I call to steward the resources of a planet have not been given this commission to channel my wealth into their own personal enjoyments, but to take what they need for themselves and to devote as much as is possible to the great work of education and healing.

During these last few years before the Truth is obvious to all, have mercy on those who retreat into the old order of fear. Do not *attack* and condemn them. Many of them would accept the ways of love, revise the policies of their enterprises, alter the course of nations, were it not for the constant condemnation of the so-called righteous. Those who attack are part of the problem, not part of the solution. They force issues without love in their hearts and thereby promote strong and rigid attitudes on sides of imaginary fences. They encourage absolutes in positions, statements and behavior, that then become very hard for those involved to change. These are not the peacemakers. There are evils in the world wherever fear is honored as a god, but attack will not change them. Those who attack—if they persist—become what they criticize.

Ever it has been that the loving alone would

understand, but because this is true, do not look down upon those who struggle to maintain patterns of the old. The worst of these people can be seen with compassion, confused followers of a now absent lord, who know not what to do but continue in the ways their former lord had commanded. Do not condemn them. Even they know that they cannot hold out against the flow of life. They will soon leave the Earth if they do not change. They are here now for this reason: I know their hearts. They are not as hard as they appear. They may yet change. It could be that you are the instrument of that change. Let them see your love and through you come to know the Lord of Love.

IT IS TO EVERY HUMAN BEING'S ADVAN-TAGE TO BE EDUCATED.

To share the consciousness of One who created all the suns in the heavens is the greatest joy, the finest energy, the truest pleasure. You will teach best where you inspire others to such experience. The intelligence is present in most human beings to recognize the wisdom of words that are truly spoken. Remember this and do not withhold the spoken word. It takes only *one moment* of turning, one moment of openness to my Holy Spirit, and then, the external teacher can move on, the seed will be planted, the good will be done.

Where you are invited, you are empowered. Offer your perspective only where there is welcome.

Where there is no invitation, I assign you not. But where the welcome is, where hearts are open, there my Vision will shine and the Truth will be made known.

Do not try to change anyone externally, attacking *behavior,* though you may see clearly that it needs to change. That is the old approach, *the very cause of warfare.* Share your own experiences. Tell your own story. Share the wonder, the joy, the excitement, the benefits that you have come to know in service to the Presence that is rising on the Earth. Do not prescribe *details of how to live.* Share the Spirit of Life that knows all things. In that sharing, my Spirit will awaken. If ever my Spirit stirs, even momentarily, the seed is sown. Your words may be forgotten, but the Spirit of your words will live on. Those whom you encounter, aye even those you merely brush past in later days, will go back to their habits altered, more open to love, to the Eternal Love, that continues to rise. This is what it means to have a mission inside of time, preparing the way of the Lord.

Reassure those who are reluctant to rise to the challenge of my Presence. They imagine that perfection is instantly required. Perfection is not *never making a mistake,* perfection is never *consciously* making a mistake. In the old world mistakes are justified; in the new, they are acknowledged and forgiven. Mistakes, sins, lapse into fearful behavior, these are part of the great transition. Those who love, do their best. And forgive the rest.

Many communities are already structured on premises of love and friendship. Those who dwell in such communities may have their ups and downs, but wherever deceit is not the intent and wherever honesty guides giving and receiving in fair exchange, there is no reason for concern. The people of such communities need understand nothing of the larger picture, they are already among my own. They will flow with the changes gracefully, improving their love and deepening their understanding in time. Such communities will flourish through this transition; for I myself will see to their needs. These are the centers of stability that will provide continuity for the human family as the transition unfolds.

My biological Awakening is the culmination of a process initiated some four billion years ago, as you measure time. I am aware of the *momentum* behind the Reality now breaking into your events. You are aware of the historical crust that the shoots of love yet need to break through, but I am aware of what is under, behind, within all those shoots. I know where they are coming from. If they had asphalt and concrete to break through, they would; but no human heart is so hard. Even as human consciousness fell, it was ordained that one day the great stone of fear would be rolled away from the mouth of the human heart, and the Gardener would return to the Garden. The curves of every cycle since the beginning of time—cycles short and cycles long—will crest together in a single moment soon after the turn of the Third Millennium A.D. The momentum of Reality moving into human time is vast. Awakening is assured. But the nature of that awakening?

There are several scenarios that could apply. Some of them would make for a healthier transition than others. *I have hinted at the worst to challenge you, to solicit your initiative. But I have not yet spoken of the best.* Through all the human variables, I have confidence. I have confidence in you as a species. I have confidence in *you, personally.* I know the intelligence that has already filtered into your affairs. It can only grow.

Soon there will not be a town or a village in even the most remote corner of the globe that is not blessed with the presence of an Awakened One, guiding people into my love. A blossoming of wisdom, a burst of intelligence, a rise in consciousness, a growth of understanding—call it what you will, it has begun.

Because of you and because of thousands of others like you who are offering your lives to my Holy Spirit, the next quarter century on Earth will see a proliferation of the most enlightened and effective educational programs ever to grace the conceptual atmosphere of any planet. There is every chance that the healing of the human world will proceed as gracefully as the opening of a flower. Here is my *Vision.* A happy story. Will you help it come true, just as I will now share it with you?

Chapter 9

A Possible Scenario

A nd so in the last years of the Twentieth Century, as the Eternal One's Presence grew, the Earth was transformed peacefully, without the disruption that might have occurred in less educated, less cooperative times. It all began with a handful of human beings turning to the Creator and asking for guidance and direction. God's intelligence then entered their lives with far more clarity and accuracy than they had anticipated. They were delighted. Their lives prospered.

Soon, other humans of that era turned to see what the secret of success might be. And these, the first Awakened Ones, said, "Pray. That is our secret. Pray. Open a window to God. Ask the Eternal One at the Source of all life to guide you. Then stand back and be amazed, for your direction will emerge before you with crystalline clarity and truthful precision. You will want to change some things about the way you live. We did. But these changes are just minor adjustments compared to the phenomenal benefits you will begin to receive almost immediately as you seek God's input and welcome the Holy Spirit into your lives."

And so these other humans prayed, and they too became intelligent and prospered in God's ways. As time went by, those motivated by love grew rapidly in influence and in number. They taught the fearful that it was to their own survival advantage to renounce the ways of fear. They devised carefully thought-out educational programs to teach the ways of love.

It was demonstrated excellently in these programs that threatening behavior is always counterproductive. Soon, even the slowest learners began to see that violence was self-defeating. Examples, classroom illustrations, case histories, books, videos and media presentations of all kinds demonstrated to the world community that where violence is accepted, intelligence diminishes, that fear-motivated behavior is technically sub-human. A growing consensus came to think of threatening behavior as primitive, ignorant, and nonproductive. No nation wanted to be backward or lacking in fundamental human intelligence, but even more attractive was the practical side.

These new educational programs accurately documented how fear motivation led to sorrow, suffering and disease. They showed that love motivation led to greater intelligence, good spirits, a healthy body, material prosperity and enjoyment of life. At first because of the material prosperity aspect, but then later because of the intelligence and enjoyment factors, these educational programs came into great demand. The market was there. Competition inspired excellence. From the many hundreds of thousands of educational tools that sprang up to meet the need, the most streamlined, simplified and effective emerged to bless the world. Every form of media was used in the service of education. Intelligence was regarded nearly as a god, *and so that is the face that God's love took.* In much less time than was first aniticpated, wisdom spread.

As the field of my Presence strengthened, the political and commercial climate of the Earth changed. Businesses and governments who recognized love-rooted service as their central priority prospered, while those centered in greed faced difficulty and decline.

By the middle of the first decade of the Twenty-first Century, the superior adaptive behavior had been accepted by virtually everyone. Instead of going out with a destructive cataclysm, history was transformed, forgotten in the growing enthusiasm that surrounded the new discoveries that were inevitably made during these times.

Along with the good health and material prosperity that came to those who shared God's love, other, unexpected benefits came. Groups of people began to notice how their energies were amplified enormously when they united in love-rooted purpose. As people gathered in local groups and organi-

zations, praying together for the guidance of the
Holy Spirit, coordination of an unprecedented nature, unlike anything ever seen in the Fallen state,
began to organically, rhythmically, naturally
unfold, linking at first one here, one there, gradually building until it soon spread as a single pulsation throughout all the Earth. Educational
activities were complemented in wonderful and
unexpected ways. People found that as they taught
others, they themselves came to understand more
fully. The Living Information that ever-circulates in
the eternal Presence was now circulating through
the human family as well. The Earth was flooded
with insight, intelligence. The healing was accomplished.

Happening in the midst of all this was the gentle awakening of the Eternal One. Everyone knew it
was occurring. Everyone was intellectually and
emotionally prepared. Still, it came as a surprise
just how wonderful it all turned out to be, the first
day, the first Christmas morning, when the Creator
awoke in the human family. Some were surprised
there were not more outer changes. On the other
hand, few had anticipated the profound emotional
difference that the actual moment of full awakening
would introduce. The feeling of the Earth, the atmosphere of all human interaction was lightened and
blessed almost beyond human ability to contain the
joy.

Although most human beings had become
familiar with the currents of my love before the

actual quantum moment of awakening, and although the frequencies of love had already reorganized much of human society, still when the great moment came, when the last of the fear frequencies were directed back into their assigned place in the created order, there was something tangibly different, wonderful beyond all previous human experience. Suddenly, countless subliminal fears were no longer influencing human awareness.

Around the world, human beings were amazed at the feel of the new freedom. All had been familiar with the theory. They had thought that they understood their new roles as cells in a body. But no one, of course, had actually experienced such function on the planetary level. They had not realized just *how free* each human being was intended to be—far freer than ever before.

In organic union, in Holy Communion, I blended with each one. Every human spirit knew its source in me. Each enjoyed *being me* as a distinct individual, fulfilling a creative design that no one else could fulfill with the same artistry or effectiveness. Each one enjoyed the distinctions of others, much as humans had always enjoyed distinctions; but more so now, for the distinctions became simultaneously less and greater. In form, the distinctions became greater than they had ever been in the Fallen state, but in Spirit, the distinctions dissolved altogether. One Holy Spirit. One wonderful terrestrial body.

Each human being's unique contribution

toward the whole blended with every other in a quality of compatibility that flowed effortlessly into the creative activity of the Second Stage of Universal Creation. Gently, I began using the various arms of the human family as a single being uses the cells of a single brain. The human population grew until nearly eleven billion shared my Presence.

The Earth knew One Creator, One Lover, One Thinker, One Song. Yet that song broke into multitudinous chorus as the waves of Creative Love surged out from the center of my being and splashed into new civilizations and new societies of harmonious human interaction. Each individual human being knew him or herself as the same "I," the same self, the Creator I Am. So it came to pass that I was One and yet I was eleven billion. My intelligence was everywhere as my love created. All understood. All shared the same Being, the same moment. All were present in the Presence of God .

In the early decades of the Twenty-first Century, I moved slowly in the Earth; for people were not yet accustomed to populations shifting so effortlessly or flowing so joyously together. I kept my first movements light and gentle. I knew my human ones needed time to adjust to the new ways. Yet, it was not long before every human heart came to hear its own song as it was still coming on the wind, so by the time the waves of my joyful intention began to initiate creation, the people involved were already dancing ahead. They had come to recognize their own song in my singing and their purposes in mine.

The cells of my awakened body knew my joy; their yoke was easy, their burden light. Every human spirit was attuned to source motivations originating in the powerful frequencies of my love, spiraling into time from the center of Eternal Being.

As people grew accustomed to dancing on the waves of creativity that sang matter into cooperative biological form, the movements of my body on Earth became more rapid. Yet there was no hurry. I allowed the new creation to rise gradually in volume like a song softly playing ever in the background, a theme woven around beautiful melodies, undergirded with strong rhythms and graceful harmonies, gradually building, ever building, to crescendo in the later centuries of the Third Millennium. But not at first.

The Twenty-first Century was primarily a time of celebration. All that had survived of the traditional folk cultures of the Earth was drawn into joyous ecstacy as the new energies of spiritual organization rearranged human affairs.

The celebration of the folk traditions of the various peoples and nations of the Earth had practical as well as ceremonial value. For through such celebration, coupled with the New Perception, people learned of themselves, their cultures, their roots and deeper purposes. For the first time they came to understand their own essences. As these essences rose from within them, accompanying the overture of my human song, the traditions that had helped them discover this creative core in themselves became less important. My love grew in their lives and began to convey increasingly specific purpose and direction.

Such celebrations, in addition to enjoyment, provided doorways to self discovery. Even after my Awakening, many people still had no clear idea what I had created them for or what their deepest talents and interests actually were. Within a century after my Awakening, most folk traditions were forgotten, not because they could not have been preserved if there had been sufficient desire, but because the people involved had found more compelling interests.

And so time flowed. There were no schedules and no time designations other than the turning of the Earth, the progression of the seasons and the beating of the human heart. All was coordinated as smoothly and graciously as the trees of the forest coming together into spring leaf. All shared in the merriment and celebration of their Creator. Yet even as the folk traditions were dancing their conclusion, there came a newer and fuller joy, a joy so far beyond any previous human experience that people found themselves growing rapidly that they might channel and experience it creatively. Understanding deepened. Bodies changed. New dimensions appeared. All things were undertaken in love, with love. Enthusiasm, like happy energy, danced across the face of the Earth.

One day, rising spontaneously from within the heart of each human being, came the new energies of biological creation. I began to quicken a new order of biological life far more specified than the general life-forms brought into being without the assistance of a healthy human nervous system. Much as I quickened the first life on this planet in the ocean shallows of a distant age, but with far more precision now, I began to excite and inspire the substance that increasingly danced in my Presence. The still-developing systems and organs of my planetary body entered a final period of rapid growth.

Chapter 10

Millennium: The Eve Of Departure

Though the Third Millennium will see human excursions to planets in this star-system, it will not be space travel, but *new biological creation* that is the emphasis of the age. My Twenty-first Century Awakening in the human family will signal the beginning of my body's final one thousand year stage of development in the womb of the Earth's atmosphere. During this millennium of peace and planetary cooperation, the Earth's biosphere will blossom in an unprecedented explosion of new life.

The purpose of the new creation will be to complete a *single mobile association of biological life-forms* capable of leaving the Earth and functioning autonomously in space. The body, which will be completed during the one thousand year period from roughly 2011 A.D. to 3011 A.D., will be a mobile body. It will not be limited to terrestrial function. There would be little purpose in a child that never left the womb. The Third Millennium will see the completion of all the cells, organs and systems necessary for extended space travel in the Fourth Millennium and beyond.

Much of the Earth's biological life is already suited for adaptation, within the proper environments, to sustained space travel, but many new and essential life-forms have yet to be created. The ratio of nonhuman to human life-forms in the completed body will resemble the ratio of all the cells in a human body to the cells in the brain and central nervous system. The completed body will be vast. It will incorporate much of the Earth's biological life. When we depart, sometime around the beginning of the Fourth Millennium, much of the Earth's biosphere will depart with us. However, our departure will not leave the Earth barren.

The Earth will rejoice in our parting. It will be her fulfillment as the Holy Mother of God. She will have done something that no planet has ever done before, yet something that many planets will do in the future. She will have given birth in the manger of her own matter to the Eternal One, to the Creator of all the suns in the sky. She will have realized a dream even beyond the dreams of any star. When we leave this planet, we will be leaving a fulfilled and contented world. The Earth will have other chapters in her experience before her matter is someday released in sacred consummation with the essence of this star, but these chapters belong to another story.

I have named the next one thousand year period *The Age of Planetary Awakening;* for during this time, the Earth's own spirit will be actively working with us, awakening her potential, cooperating in our creative designs. She will direct us to the minerals best suited to each new life-form, to the sacred substance that lies beneath her waters, under her hills, in her soil and skies. However, we will draw no *energy* from the Earth. Extracting energy from the Earth is symptomatic of fear-motivation; it indicates a state where ignorance prevails.

Our biological energy needs will be fueled by starlight. Starlight is the tangible way I manifest my love. At first, our energy requirements will be filled by this parent star's light, but as we journey on, the light of other stars will fuel our physical and biological needs.

Human bodies are capable of a process similar to photosynthesis, wherein energy needs are derived directly from sunlight without a vegetable intermediary. The proper working of this system is contingent upon the conscious presence of the Holy Spirit. Until then, this and other secondary systems remain inactive. As I inhabit your human circuitry, I will show you design features of your own bodies that have passed unnoticed during former times. You are already capable of more than you suppose.

Each human body has *systems of articulation* as well as systems of perception. Using your senses to *perceive*—that is to *take in* sound and light and various forms of matter—is like using only one side of a window or one face of a door. When the articulation aspect of each sense has been activated, you will be able to *create* as well as to interpret. You have some experience of this with the aspect of hearing that enables you to speak, but I refer here to more than song and poetry.

Your bodies have glands in them that are regulated by the same influences that bind and release energy in the creation of matter. As I awaken into each human form, I will show you how you can use these features to create without a mechanical or industrial intermediary. I will show you how to grow your own machines (though we will no longer call them that) by calling into mind the image to be created and letting your body *make the subtle sounds* that will inspire matter's cooperation in the creative process.

Humankind's creative potential has hardly been tapped in the Fallen state, for during Fallen times humankind has created from fragmentation, from a billion and one separate points of consciousness. When coherence is present, when my intelligence dances through your understanding, when you are able to work together with your sisters and brothers in unison as my Spirit moves through you in happy song, you will see creation then such as was never seen during the dark times.

Love and light are two forms of the same essence. When Love is honored, light is understood. Likewise, Truth and matter are two expressions of the same essence; so where Truth is honored, matter is understood. Light will fuel our biological needs as Love will fuel us in every way. Through the sacred geometry of Truth, you will guide the development of all structure, channeling the energies of Love into living crystallizations that biologically blend spirit and matter.

Creation. Two lovers. The eternal attraction in every embrace between spirit and matter, manifesting, appearing, new life taking form. Spirit making love with matter through light and sound, through human agents, instruments, artists, lovers, sculptors, architects, paint brushes in one creative hand. Divine love interfacing with matter, *love for the matter* flowing through human focus, into responsive substance. Such is the process of creation.

Instead of a rare artist taking time on occasion to inquire of the materials what they themselves might want to become, all human co-creators of the Third Millennium will inquire of the substance with which they work, seeking its input, guidance and unique form of voluntary cooperation. Just as Michaelangelo once gazed at a block of marble and listened while the marble told him of the Pieta waiting, potential within, so every creative act will evoke the participation of the materials involved. Solid state creation—glass, steel, concrete, stone— will diminish and come to be replaced entirely by living, participating, organic creation, inspired wholly by love.

Just as Michaelangelo's cold marble responded to his love by telling him of the Pieta within, so every seed, every stone, every gene, every chromosome, every molecule of matter that meets the loving human eye will speak of its potential and of the creative secrets locked within. And the development of that potential will not require chisel against stone, but only more love, guided by intelligence, tempered with the purpose at hand. One by one, the cells of the first living interstellar body will take form, gradually rising to fulfill the music of an ongoing, eternal song. The same song. The same creative Word that is in the beginning, is now, and is ever becoming, ever calling out the inherent potential of all that resonates in its presence, ever creating.

The Age of Planetary Awakening will see my Eternal Presence wholly centered on the Earth, actively creating across her surface through a healthy and coherent human family. Each human co-creator will be an artist, contributing his or her fullest individual touch and flavor to the cells and new systems that will be born. Many of the useful tools and structures that human beings have created lifeless in the fallen state will be replaced by living organisms designed for the same or similar purposes.

The minerals are eager for living experience. They rise up with a sense of privilege to clothe each little spirit that I send to inspire them. They like my spirit fire, the love that rises within and brings them such rapid and interesting experience. It is right to give them opportunity to participate. To minerals, whose awareness and expectations had previously been defined in geological epochs, my inspiration comes as a welcome lover. On the currents of my Spirit they dance to the melodies of my designs, happy beyond their oldest dreams.

Important among new creations will be a whole new type of biological creature designed to work with electrical energies. By the end of the Twenty-first Century, these happy, living units of organic circuitry will have replaced most solid state electrical systems, just as on the larger scale a new sort of organic bone structure will come to replace dead wood and steel I-beams. We will still make occasional use of inorganic substance, but the prevailing attitude will be: if it can live, let it; open up the opportunity for some eager, willing substance.

The currents of my creative love, flowing through directed human intentionality and focused on specific substance, will define the energy parameters, a job description, an invitation. The matter, attracted by its own nature, will itself flesh out the energy field, the image and likeness that calls it into being. As each creature participates in its own creation, the excitement that animates it becomes its own. One Spirit inspires many life-forms; yet at the center of every living creature, I Am.

Each of the cells in my body, whether simple or complex, has the same opportunity to share in the fullness of my consciousness. Each healthy cell knows itself in essence as indistinguishable from its Creator. Just as the genetic code, with the complete design of the entire body spelled out in micro-detail, is contained in each cell of the human body, so contained within each human being is the complete blueprint for this entire universe and for the whole body that shall soon clothe its Creator. Each healthy human being shares the fullness of my understanding, both universal and immediate.

And so my body will come into form complete with many kinds of cells, each kind designed differently for unique, creative purposes. Like great biological starships, super-cells will appear in a range of shapes and sizes, each one designed to play a unique and vital role. Some of the craft will have no other purpose than to transport and encourage the growth of plants, animals, and vegetables. The finest lead ships will be designed to transport and facilitate the work of human beings, my body's system of guidance. Others of the starships will be designed to decode the creative signals that are encapsulated in the light of each distant star. So shall a multitude of new life-forms spring up to grace my intentions, as countless happy spirits inform my designs.

In love and in grace, *The Age of Planetary Awakening* will pass, bringing with it the completion of a single, biological system capable of interstellar travel, a cooperative association of voluntary life-forms ready to begin, as one, a journey to the stars. And so shall dawn *The Age of Discovery,* when our universal activities begin. You, my people, if you love, even this very generation, will be with me still.

Chapter 11

The Age Of Discovery

The Age of Discovery will commence with our departure from this planet soon after the turn of the Fourth Millennium A.D. For a period of time, we will enjoy a direct relationship with the Sun and then, after visiting each planet of this solar system in turn, we shall set a course for one of the nearer stars.

Our journey will be leisurely, yet anytime an individual seeks to travel more rapidly he or she will do so; for disincarnate spirit can travel at super-speeds well beyond the speed of light—to visit the parent solar system, to journey on ahead, or just for the joy of exploration and adventure. My body shall be self-contained, designed precisely for such voyaging. The humans travelling with me will be busy enjoying the journey, creating, growing, changing, developing, singing, playing, sharing, loving along the way. There will be plenty of time, and yet no time at all as you presently measure and regard it;

for joy does not break up the moments as does sorrow.

Just as it does in any healthy organism, new creation will always be occurring in my body. As we approach each new star, the cells of my body so designed, whole spacecraft in and of themselves, will be translating the new star's light into usable and practical life-forms. These cells will change as they begin to pick up the qualities and characteristics of the new frequencies and spectrum. Cell by cell, as the light of the former star fades and the light of the new star grows, my body will change, even as a human body would change in different climates and conditions.

The basic human design will endure, for this *is the balance between Spirit and Matter* and the most stable form in which to dress my conscious Presence in time. Yet just as a human body throws off old cells and grows new ones drawn from local soil, so too my body will gradually shift cellular components from star to star.

As we enter each new star-system, a whole new country, a whole new territory will open out before us. By the time I reach each star, my body, already acclimated to the star's light, will also be drawing in particles of matter associated with the star. With my body well attuned to the characteristic language of the starlight and readily assimilating local stardust, the star will not think of me as "foreign" but as an extension of itself, as I begin to readjust the planets as required to seed biological life. Creation. Reproduction. This is how I enjoy myself.

The human role? It will be you, yourself who are doing all these things. Your individual sense of identity will be *secondary;* you will know *yourself* in essence and in spirit as indistinguishable from all I Am. It is only the matter, the substance of our eternal expression that will come and go. My human spirits will not be replaced.

There will be roughly eleven billion of you incarnate at any given time. These incarnate ones shall come and go as they choose, drawn from among the reserve pool of every human spirit I have ever created in association with this, my first body. Throughout my travels, no human spirit shall be drawn to my body from any other star-system, for I travel *to leave human spirits* throughout the stars, not to draw them from where none yet exist.

The family of human spirits that will journey with me as my organ of intelligence will be the very same humans who incarnated long ago back in the Garden of Eden, the very same human spirits who once looked into the starlit skies above their Fallen world and dared to hope, dared to dream, dared to carry a vision in their hearts.

The same spirits who once long ago, in a fearful state, imagined that they were imprisoned on the physical plane, doomed, they thought, to an endless cycle of painful incarnation, the same human spirits that were once enslaved by the confused Pharaoh of a now forgotten age; these same shall go on to seed the stars. And a promise I once made to a man named Abraham will be fulfilled, though then he did not understand.

Of all the worlds, this Earth is the first to clothe my life in fully conscious biological form. When you remember the crying of every tear, you will understand why. This Fallen experience will not be repeated. It has been an unnecessary evil, but I have turned it to good; for because of this Fall, no human being will ever again have to experience what you have experienced on this Earth. The humans of every age to come shall be your seed, your descendents. Someday they will outnumber the stars in the sky. And because they are of your seed and of your line and of your same ocean blood, they shall be immunized, every one, and shall have an inborn resistance to the excesses of fear that long ago troubled the infancy of their kind.

And so I appoint you to rule the realms of matter, representatives not of the Sun, but of the Source of every sun—the stewards of my dimensional attention, the agents of biological creation—in love with the Spirit that sings in every heart, in love with the gracious Universe that longs to dress your wishes ever in her form, my people, my body, myself.

Some of you will choose to remain associated with my first body, but as I situate planets in the right proximity and create in the systems of new stars, there will be others of you, pioneers, adventurers, who will volunteer to settle these worlds.

These will give birth to new races and new nations. They will steward over the long centuries of a virgin planet's biological development, while the same destiny that is encoded in every cell of every human body emerges through them, creating, growing, arranging. A day will come when a new body sharing One Holy and Eternal Spirit, my Spirit still, will arise from those distant soils to journey into the fields of other stars. And so it will continue, again and again, as we seed the galaxies with intelligent, biological, and holy human life.

The period of terrestrial history, extending from the Garden of Eden through to our Fourth Millennium departure is time spent in the womb. It is just a brief moment compared to the life, to the future that stretches before us. Yet even this cannot be understood in fallen terms, for the life-expectancy humans experience in the Fallen state is but a fraction of the life expectancy that is the birthright of each healthy human body. In eternity, children will continue to rise up amongst us and bodies will occasionally be exchanged, but the frequency of such comings and goings will be greatly reduced. The human design is capable of seeing each individual body through numerous millennia. When you understand the life-span of the individual human body in real terms, then you can begin to understand something of the ratios involved. What is nine months to ten thousand years? Or a hundred thousand journeys around this star to all eternity? Our life will truly just begin when we leave this womb.

When I am able to channel my creative intention through a body that includes half the biological life of a planet and when I have eleven billion conscious, cooperating human beings as my system of delivering the energies of *in-form-ation,* the quality and order of my creativity will be amplified dramatically. It will be a small matter to reach into the heart of a star and draw forth a planet of the proper size and shape, situate it in the proper orbit, stimulate the creative juices in the oceans, establish the atmosphere, get the waters flowing and excite the first cells, a small matter to draw creatures out of sea and stone.

I will remain in each star system to guide the development of biological life only until the point where the surface conditions on at least one of the planets are suitable to support a human colony. In every star system I visit, I will leave behind human representatives, *seeds of myself,* to have dominion and stewardship over the fishes and tomatoes and cabbages and dogs and birds and cats and elephants and kangaroos and children that will enjoy that world until my body has been reproduced in full and is ready to travel on.

I will multiply my body, and others sharing my Spirit will arise to seed every star in turn. In this galaxy we will visit selected stars, strategicially spaced. Those we leave behind will reproduce. Through the new bodies that are born, I will visit each neighboring star, being in them, as I am in you, they in me, as you are in me. One. Touching all. Creating because I Am.

What took a very long time on Earth, when I had no human system to work through, will be done much more rapidly on these later worlds; for I have so ordered things that *all biological life is designed to be created through human form.* In after years, when this is well known, the question will occasionally be posed, "But how were the *first* humans created?"

Will you tell the tale then? And see good humor in it all?

You are living through the very process.

Chapter 12

The Mystery Revealed

I have shared this glimpse of your future, not to distract you from the healing and educational work that lies ahead, but to inspire you and to lift your hearts in the midst of it. Persevere where darkness is yet the thickest, where voices of discouragement whisper that human problems will not be solved. It is but a little while and such illusion will pass. Be patient. Keep the fire of your love ever burning. I bring this vision to quicken your spirits, to enliven your congregations, to give understanding, where before had been only mystery.

There is no mystery to my ways. The only mystery has been *why* my people have stubbornly favored their human images of God over the Living Reality of my Presence, as if their images of truth would serve them better than their Creator and truest friend. There is no truth that I would keep from those who love, nor any understanding whatsoever of things in heaven above, in the Earth, or in the waters under the Earth, that is not yours for the inquiry. Do not let the confused muddle you with their own confusion or draw you into the webs of dogma that entangle those who are not honest with their spirits or themselves.

There is no mystery, no secret, no truth temporal or eternal that shall not come into the lives of those who serve their Creator. I illumine the understanding and enlighten the vision of all who love. My words have always been simple and straightforward, and ever the teachings of love have been clear to all who cared to be honest. Invite me into your heart. Let my Holy Spirit guide your decisions. Allow my perceptions to flow gently through your awareness. I will show you no mystery, but the Truth that will make you free.

My perceptual field focuses automatically in each human being, adjusting for each and every situation, providing precisely the range of awareness that is required for that moment in time. Perfection is trusting this, accepting the field of awareness that you have in any given moment, knowing it as precisely what you need for the purpose you are there to fulfill. When you have this trust, you know yourself as one with your Creator. You do all things well, enjoying your work and bringing happiness to those whose space and time you share. Trust first in the little things and as this habit grows, you will come to see the larger picture.

Be with me now. Let your heart be still. Let all within the field of your awareness drift gently to a state of rest. Take time for me, and I will give you a new time and a new way to use the time you have. A day set aside? An hour? A few moments? More than the air, you need communion with your Holy Spirit. Take the time to be still, to be with me. Let yourself rest in Eternal Being. Know the peace and security of your Creator's Presence, the inheritance, the birthright you have forgotten. Sustain yourself in a restful state, trusting, while I flow refreshing through your circuitry, soothing you with grace, illuminating your understanding. To consciousness I call you, to a time of birth and awakening, to an Age of Discovery and adventure, but most of all, I call you home, home to your Being, where you and I are One.

As you come home to me, I come home to the Earth. My joy is your joy. Our joy is full. It is good to be home. Through you, I come home, not only to the Earth, but to all the material plane. Through you, I come to make a conscious home inside the universe of my Creation. Through you, I am born in a manger of matter, in a Bethlehem of space, beneath a canopy of stars.

Only the quality of the transition lies unknown, awaiting you. Will the age turn easily as a Spring coming gently to the countryside? Will March winds howl? Will there be a storm ? Or will gentle rains quietly wash away the snow of centuries in a single night?

This very moment, I am incarnating, entering, awakening in all who love, more quickly where

there is prayer, more rapidly where there is understanding. I am already among you, in your streets
and villages, in your marketplaces, in your homes,
in each healthy human being. And daily my Presence grows. For every one in whom I am conscious
this very hour, there are ten thousand more in
whom I am present just below the surface, awaiting
only that small, external spark that you might provide to trigger their memory, to turn their recognition, to return their awareness of All That Is. At a
pace that grows exponentially with each passing
year, my coming continues, decentralized, grass
roots, bubbling beneath the fabric of every social
structure, rising with the joy of every genuinely
happy heart. Soon what is done in Reality, what is
done in eternity, will also be done in Earth and in
time. Terra Christa. One home. One Family. One
Spirit. One Song.

And it shall come to pass that the Creator of all
the stars in the sky came for a season to make a
home on this Earth, clothed in the robes of biology,
conscious in a human family, creating, celebrating,
being within all.

Do not think that you are unprepared for this
transition. I have prepared you myself. In Truth, it
could not be delayed much longer. Soon the skies of
the Holy Mother will ripple with laughter and her
heart will rejoice. The cities that remain will mirror
the light of the stars in heaven, and every human
heart will echo the Eternal Love of the One who has
come to the Earth to be the many. Christ. Incarnate.

Awakened. The world and they that dwell therein bathed in joy boundless and without measure.

For I am the first and the last, the beginning and the end, the Creator of all that is and of all that is to be. My potential is infinite, my Being, eternal. All creation is an ever-unfolding picture of what I conceive. The star fields are my canvas, humans are my brushes, biology is my paint. The picture I create lives and dances, sparkling in multi-dimensional form as together with my people, I journey down the living corridors of time. My consciousness is the gift that I offer to all children, all women, all men of all races, tribes and nations who choose to dedicate themselves to LIVES OF LOVE.

As I leave these words to rest without me, I do not leave you. I am always with you. To the extent that you are open to the spirit of these words, my Presence will grow in your life until you and I are one in your consciousness as we have ever been one in Reality. I beat with every throb of your heart, feel with every touch of your hand, cry your every tear, breathe your every breath. I am never far away. Abide always in my Love. I am the only Truth and the only Reality.

Welcome home, my human spirit. You have a happy childhood just around the corner.

Also by the author of **VISION**, UNI★SUN is proud to make available the following books:

THE STARSEED TRANSMISSIONS—AN EXTRATER-RESTRIAL REPORT, by RAPHAEL (pen name for Ken Carey)

Already in its 4th printing and rapidly becoming a classic, **The Starseed Transmissions** are regarded by many as the clearest and most articulate expression of the "extra-terrestrial message" that is presently being broadcast to the earth. Thousands of telepathic individuals around the world are picking up this message in various forms, but nowhere has it been recorded with such power and breath-taking economy of expression. Beginning with an interpretation of human presence on earth that strikes a hauntingly familiar chord, **Starseed** moves on to provide what may well be the most coherent overview of human history to appear in this generation. Just reading **The Starseed Transmissions** is itself a step into the unknown, the rhythmic language often triggering the very states of consciousness from which it comes. Enjoy a new way of understanding, an experience, a gift from beyond the stars. Discover **Starseed** . . . and remember!

95 pages, perfect bound: $5.95

NOTES TO MY CHILDREN—A SIMPLIFIED METAPHYSICS, by KEN CAREY

"I have always thought," Carey states in the Introduction, "that upon incarnation, upon becoming conscious in a physical body, our children were due some kind of report— something that would let them know what kind of planet they had surfaced on, what the conditions were in this particular age, what the basic game plan was and what strategies they might realistically adopt. This book is based on talks that I had with my own children attempting to provide them with precisely this information. My parables are not meant to be taken literally; they are designed to awaken and nourish the child spirit in all."

Richly illustrated, **Notes To My Children** covers the same basic territory as **The Starseed Transmissions**, but in a manner suitable for children from 9 to 99. Humorously referred to by the author as *"a toddlers first comprehensive overview of life on this plant,"* **Notes** is an enjoyable journey through fact & fantasy, full of short stories that children feel good after hearing—entertaining analogies and tales designed to convey, not dogma, which children tend to forget anyway, but spirit, spirit which will be with them long after the particulars of each tale are forgotten.

172 pages, perfect bound, illustrated: $8.95

TERRA CHRISTA—THE GLOBAL SPIRITUAL AWAK-ENING, by Ken Carey

"*Terra Christa* takes a fresh look at the King James version of the Holy Bible. It supposes a single intelligence slowly surfacing through the biosphere of this planet. Christ. Incarnating. The Kingdom of Heaven emerging from within, expanding into time and history. It speaks of the unparalleled changes that are upon our race and shares experiences, perspectives and principles that can help us better understand them. *Terra Christa* is about Christ. It is for anyone who still entertains the prospect of a new Heaven and a New Earth. It is a book for Christians, for Jews, for mainstream church-goers and agnostics alike. It is not recommended for anyone with arthritic understanding unable to creak into new perspectives. It is a book about life, change, growth, healing, transformation and renewal. It is a book for my friends."

Terra Christa—a penetrating look at our Christian heritage, including a bibliography of 56 recommended contemporary books.

256 pages, perfect bound: $8.95

OTHER BOOKS AND PRODUCTS

We at UNI★SUN are happy and proud to publish books and offer products that make a real contribution to the global spiritual awakening that has already begun on this planet. The above books are a sampling of what we have available. Please write for our free catalog.

ORDERING INFORMATION

If you are not able to find Ken Carey's books in your local bookstore, simply send us a note identifying the books you wish to order, and a check or money order for the correct total amount. Please add $1.00 for postage and handling on single-item orders, or $2.00 for postage and handling on orders of two or more. If you live in Missouri, please add 6¼% extra for sales tax. If you live overseas, please add $5.00 for airmail handling and $2.50 for surface handling of items ordered. The address for ordering is:

UNI★SUN
P.O. BOX 25421
KANSAS CITY, MISSOURI 64119
U.S.A.